Finding Earthlike Planets

Liz Kruesi

www.av2books.com

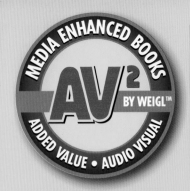

AV² provides enriched content that supplements and complements this book. Weigl's AV² books strive to create inspired learning and engage young minds in a total learning experience.

Your AV² Media Enhanced books come alive with...

Audio
Listen to sections of the book read aloud.

Key Words
Study vocabulary, and complete a matching word activity.

Video
Watch informative video clips.

Quizzes
Test your knowledge.

Embedded Weblinks
Gain additional information for research.

Slide Show
View images and captions, and prepare a presentation.

Try This!
Complete activities and hands-on experiments.

... and much, much more!

Go to **www.av2books.com**, and enter this book's unique code.

BOOK CODE

AVN28959

AV² by Weigl brings you media enhanced books that support active learning.

Published by AV² by Weigl
350 5th Avenue, 59th Floor
New York, NY 10118
Website: www.av2books.com

Library of Congress Cataloging-in-Publication Data

Names: Kruesi, Liz, author.
Title: Finding earthlike planets / Liz Kruesi.
Description: New York, NY : AV2 by Weigl, [2019] | Series: Space exploration | Audience: Grade 7 to 8. | Includes bibliographical references and index.
Identifiers: LCCN 2018053511 (print) | LCCN 2018055218 (ebook) | ISBN 9781489698247 (Multi User ebook) | ISBN 9781489698254 (Single User ebook) | ISBN 9781489698223 (hardcover : alk. paper) | ISBN 9781489698230 (softcover : alk. paper)
Subjects: LCSH: Extrasolar planets--Juvenile literature. | Extrasolar planets--Detection--Juvenile literature. | Life on other planets--Juvenile literature.
Classification: LCC QB820 (ebook) | LCC QB820 .K785 2019 (print) | DDC 523.2/4--dc23
LC record available at https://lccn.loc.gov/2018053511

Printed in Guangzhou, China
1 2 3 4 5 6 7 8 9 0 23 22 21 20 19

032019
112318

Project Coordinator: Heather Kissock   Designer: Ana María Vidal

Every reasonable effort has been made to trace ownership and to obtain permission to reprint copyright material. The publishers would be pleased to have any errors or omissions brought to their attention so that they may be corrected in subsequent printings.

Weigl acknowledges Alamy, iStock, NASA/JPL-Caltech, and Shutterstock as its primary image suppliers for this title.

First published by North Star Editions in 2018.

CONTENTS

Many of the first exoplanets scientists discovered were huge gas giants.

Chapter 1

Unexpected Planets

In the 1980s, Earth and the other planets **orbiting** the Sun were the only planets known in the universe. Since then, astronomers have found thousands of planets circling other stars. These planets are called extrasolar planets, or exoplanets for short. Astronomers had discovered more than 3,800 exoplanets by 2018. Some scientists have found signs that there may be even more planets outside our solar system. However, more research is still needed to confirm that these exoplanets exist.

Astronomers found the first two exoplanets in 1992. These exoplanets look nothing like Earth. They orbit a dead star. When a star dies, its center sometimes collapses into a **dense**, glowing cinder. This type of leftover star is very different from the Sun. Scientists were surprised to find planets orbiting these remnants.

Three years later, scientists found an exoplanet moving around a star similar to the Sun. But this exoplanet is quite different from Earth. The exoplanet travels around its star in only four days. That means it orbits very close to its star. Because it is so close to its star, the exoplanet is much hotter than Earth. In addition, the exoplanet weighs as much as Jupiter. That means it is more than 300 times as **massive** as Earth.

This type of large, hot planet is known as a hot Jupiter. During the next decade, astronomers found many other large, hot exoplanets. Some are so close to their stars that their surfaces are hot enough to melt iron.

KELT-9b (right), the hottest exoplanet discovered so far, is even warmer than some stars.

The Hubble Space Telescope orbits 353 miles (569 kilometers) above Earth's surface.

In the mid-2000s, scientists began finding large exoplanets that are farther from their stars. Some of these planets were much farther from their stars than Pluto is from the Sun. These exoplanets were found using the Hubble Space Telescope. The Hubble Space Telescope was launched into space in 1990. It has been orbiting Earth ever since. As it orbits, the telescope takes pictures of planets, stars, and other objects in space.

The **Hubble** weighs **24,500** pounds (11,110 kilograms). That is as much as two grown elephants.

In April 2018, the **Hubble Space Telescope** spotted the most **distant star** ever seen. It was **9 billion light years** away from Earth. At the speed of light, it would take 9 billion years to get there!

Because the telescope is above Earth's **atmosphere**, the pictures are much clearer than pictures taken from Earth's surface. Scientists study the pictures to learn about outer space. Sometimes, they find exoplanets. In the pictures, the exoplanets look like very faint glowing objects around the stars.

So far, Earth is the only planet scientists know of that has life. But discoveries of the 2010s came closer to finding planets that are similar to Earth. A few of these planets are the same size as Earth. Some have signs of an atmosphere. They may even have water. Water was critical for the development of life on Earth. Scientists now know of more than 50 exoplanets that may be able to support life.

The exoplanet GJ 436b is approximately the same size as Neptune.

Chapter 2

Shifting Starlight

To find most exoplanets, scientists look at changes in starlight. A planet does not create its own light. Instead, it reflects light from the star it orbits. Scientists can sometimes look for changes in starlight to find exoplanets. Because of **gravity**, a planet and its star pull on each other. Gravity's effect on two objects depends on each object's mass. For example, the Sun is 300,000 times more massive than Earth.

The Sun's pull on Earth causes Earth to orbit. Earth also pulls on the Sun. But Earth is tiny compared to the Sun. Its pull does not have much of an effect. The Sun does not move nearly as much as Earth does.

Most exoplanets are much less massive than the stars they orbit. For this reason, an exoplanet's pull is so small that astronomers will not see the star move. But the exoplanet's pull makes the starlight appear a slightly different color. Scientists can detect this change even from far away. The change tells scientists that an exoplanet is pulling at a star.

Scientists can study these changes in starlight to determine an exoplanet's mass. Exoplanets that are more massive cause larger changes. Less-massive exoplanets cause smaller changes. When the first exoplanets were discovered, scientists used this method. It helped them determine that the planets were as massive as Jupiter. Jupiter is 318 times as massive as Earth.

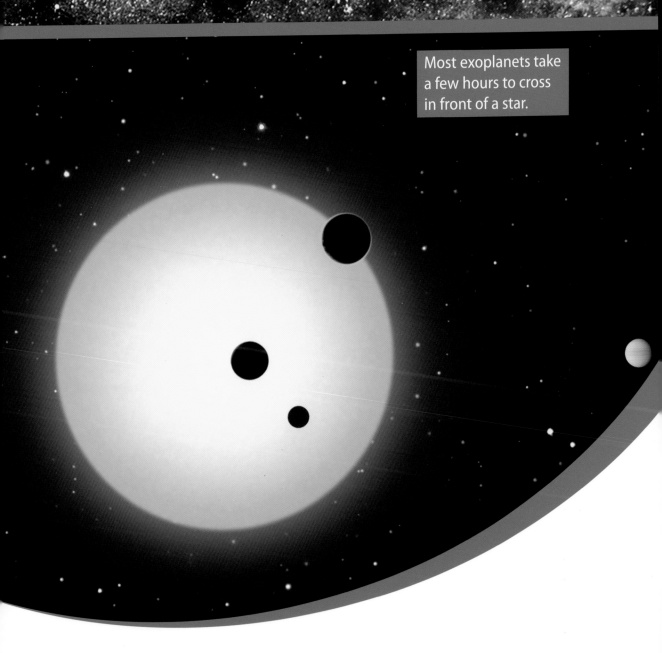

Most exoplanets take a few hours to cross in front of a star.

The strength of gravity also depends on the distance between a planet and its star. An exoplanet that is near its star pulls on the star much more than a similar-sized exoplanet that is farther away. Its pull causes a greater change to the starlight. By studying the starlight, scientists can estimate how far an exoplanet is from its star.

By the mid-2000s, scientists had found a few hundred exoplanets. But most were too massive to be much like Earth. Plus, compared with the stars they orbit, most exoplanets give off very little light. So, it is rare for exoplanets to be spotted directly. Astronomers needed a different method to find earthlike exoplanets.

The Kepler Space Telescope was 15.3 feet (4.7 m) long. Kepler was retired in October 2018 and replaced with the Transitory Exoplanet Survey Satellite (TESS).

The Kepler Space Telescope made this possible. This large telescope was launched into space in 2009. It orbited the Sun and looked out at stars across the galaxy. Scientists used the Kepler space telescope to find smaller exoplanets.

As an exoplanet passed between its star and the telescope, the exoplanet blocked a small amount of the star's light. The Kepler space telescope detected these tiny dips in starlight. When scientists noticed regular dips in a star's light, they knew an exoplanet was present.

To calculate how far that exoplanet is from the star, scientists measure how often the dips happen. Each dip means the exoplanet has completed one orbit. A planet that is farther away will take longer to move around its star. For this reason, exoplanets with bigger orbits have less-frequent dips in light.

Astronomers can also estimate the exoplanet's size. To do this, they measure how long the planet takes to cross in front of, or transit, its star. And they study how much light the exoplanet blocks when it passes between the star and a telescope. A larger exoplanet will block more starlight as it crosses in front of the star. A smaller exoplanet will block less light.

An exoplanet's distance from its star also affects how much light it blocks. An exoplanet will block more light if it is close to its star. An exoplanet that is farther away will block less light. Based on the size of the dip in starlight and the size of the star, scientists can calculate the planet's **radius**.

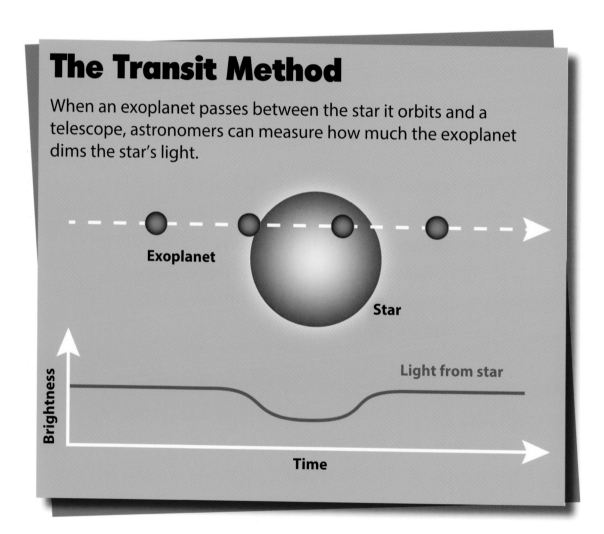

The Transit Method

When an exoplanet passes between the star it orbits and a telescope, astronomers can measure how much the exoplanet dims the star's light.

Exoplanet

Star

Light from star

Brightness

Time

Timeline

Every year, scientists discover more earthlike planets as technology improves.

1990 — The Hubble Space Telescope was launched.

1992 — The first exoplanet was found orbiting around PSR B1257+12.

Planet GJ436b was discovered. — **2004**

2009 — The Kepler Space Telescope mission was launched.

The *Cassini* space **probe**, which was launched to study Saturn and its system, crashed into Saturn. This ended its 20-year mission. — **2017**

More than 3,700 exoplanets in total have been located. The Kepler mission was retired, and the TESS mission was launched. — **2018**

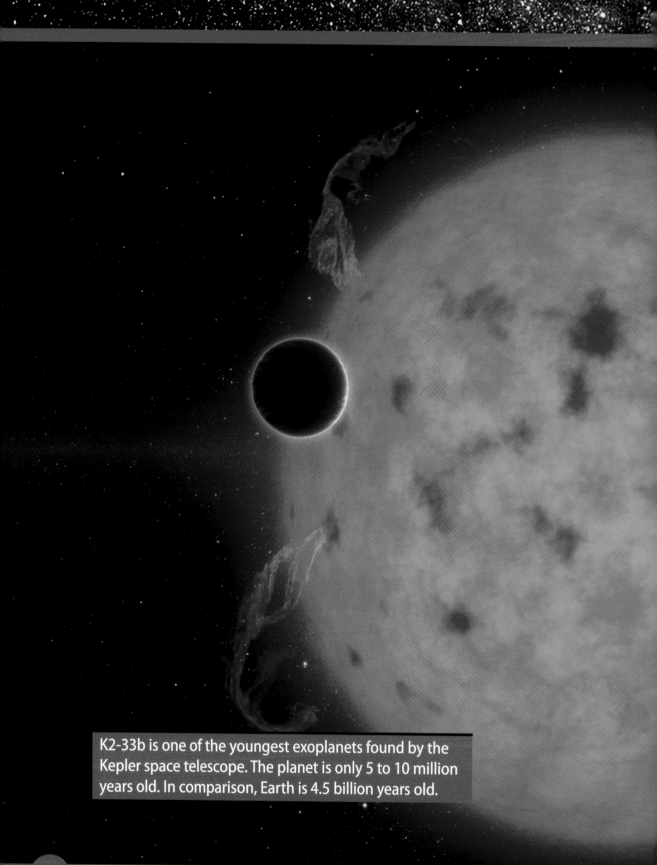

K2-33b is one of the youngest exoplanets found by the Kepler space telescope. The planet is only 5 to 10 million years old. In comparison, Earth is 4.5 billion years old.

Chapter 3

Multiple Methods

Most known exoplanets were found using the Kepler telescope. However, scientists use other methods, too. Sometimes, when an exoplanet passes between a distant star and Earth, astronomers can measure how light from that star is bent by gravity.

This strange effect works a bit like a magnifying glass. Suppose an exoplanet passes between a telescope and a faraway star. The planet sometimes bends that star's light. This causes the star to appear brighter for a short time. Astronomers have found approximately 50 exoplanets using this method.

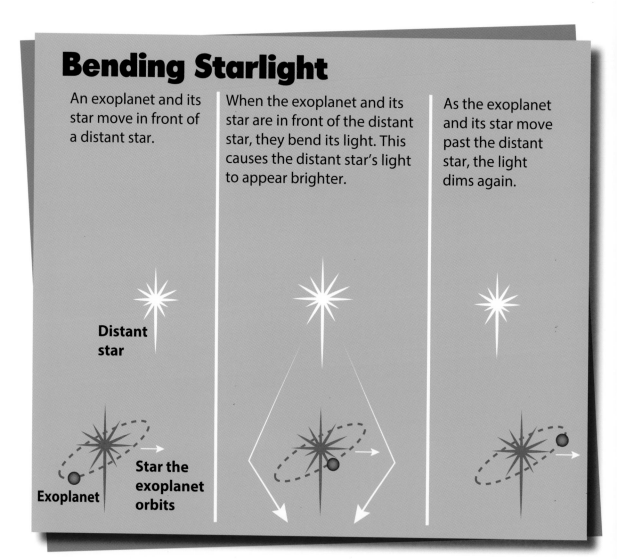

Bending Starlight

An exoplanet and its star move in front of a distant star.

When the exoplanet and its star are in front of the distant star, they bend its light. This causes the distant star's light to appear brighter.

As the exoplanet and its star move past the distant star, the light dims again.

Distant star

Exoplanet

Star the exoplanet orbits

Scientists have also found exoplanets by looking at photographs. Most planets are too faint compared to their stars to be seen in photos. However, astronomers have found approximately 40 planets in pictures. These huge planets are very far from their stars. They can be hundreds of times the distance Earth is from the Sun.

Unlike other exoplanets scientists have found, these large exoplanets are warm and young. Astronomers think these planets are only a few million years old. The young, warm planets give off more infrared light than older, cooler planets. That light makes these young planets more visible to cameras. Future technology may make it possible to discover many more exoplanets by studying photographs.

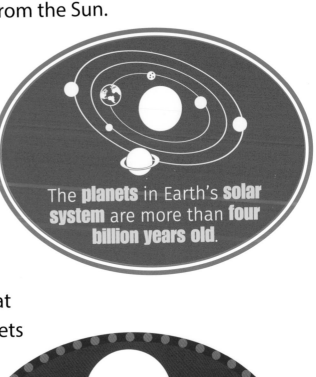

The **planets** in Earth's **solar system** are more than **four billion years old**.

The largest **exoplanets** are called **Super-Jupiters**. One of the largest is **20 times** larger than Jupiter.

John Asher Johnson

Astronomer John Asher Johnson studied physics in college. He began studying exoplanets in graduate school. Johnson finished graduate school in 2007. Two years later, he became a professor at the California Institute of Technology.

In 2013, Johnson joined Harvard University in Massachusetts. He leads a research group called ExoLab. The group uses many techniques to find and study exoplanets. One of the tools they use is a group of telescopes called MINERVA. These four telescopes are located in Arizona. Each telescope is 27.6 inches (70 centimeters) in **diameter**. The telescopes can each look in a separate direction. Or, they can work together to give scientists a better view of one space object. Computers connect the telescopes and send data back to Harvard.

Johnson is also part of the team of scientists who use the Kepler space telescope to find exoplanets. After an exoplanet is found, these scientists study it. They try to learn about its mass and orbit. Johnson also researches the stars that exoplanets orbit. He analyzes the stars' mass, brightness, and size. Johnson studies the relationship between a star's traits and the exoplanets that orbit it.

Chapter 4

The Search for an Earth Twin

By 2017, scientists had found hundreds of exoplanets that are approximately the same size as Earth. But to really be an Earth twin, an exoplanet must have more than a similar size. Its characteristics must match Earth's. The planet would need to be dense and rocky. It would need liquid water and some dry land.

Kepler-10c (right) is a rocky exoplanet that is part of the Kepler-10 system. It weighs 17 times as much as Earth and is twice as large.

To know if an exoplanet is similar to Earth, scientists need to know how dense the planet is. Astronomers start by measuring the exoplanet's mass and diameter. They use these numbers to calculate the exoplanet's density. A rocky planet is denser than a planet made of gas. So, an earthlike planet would be made of solid, rocky material.

An Earth twin would need liquid water. This means the planet must not be too cold or too hot. It would also need an atmosphere. Most of these characteristics depend on how far the exoplanet is from its star.

Stars send out energy in the form of heat and light. The amount of heat and light the exoplanet receives depends on its distance from the star. Earth orbits the Sun at a distance known as the habitable zone. At this distance, water can remain a liquid. It is far enough from the Sun that Earth is not too hot. But it is close enough that the planet is not too cold. An Earth twin would need to be in its star's habitable zone. For example, a rocky exoplanet called HD 219134 b is a similar size to Earth. But it orbits its star in just three days. This means it is very close to its star. The planet's surface would be much too hot for liquid water.

HD 219134 b is 1.6 times the size of Earth, but its surface is extremely hot. It is uninhabitable as a result. Habitable planets are often called Goldilocks planets because they are just right for things to live and grow.

For water to stay liquid, the planet must also be protected from stellar flares. Stellar flares are particles emitted by stars. The Sun is a middle-aged star of average temperature, so its flares are relatively small. But other stars emit powerful flares. These flares could change the exoplanet's surface. A planet's atmosphere stops the particles before they reach the planet's surface. On Earth, the atmosphere also protects the surface from harmful cosmic radiation, or high-energy particles that come from astronomical sources other than the Sun.

Earth's atmosphere keeps the planet's temperature relatively constant. Planets without atmospheres have bigger temperature changes. For example, Mercury does not have an atmosphere. Mercury's temperature can reach 800 degrees Fahrenheit (427° Celsius) on the side facing the Sun. The planet's other side gets as cold as −290 degrees Fahrenheit (−179°C). Water will not stay liquid if the temperature changes too much. Such extreme conditions are also unlikely to support life. To truly be an Earth twin, an exoplanet would likely need an atmosphere.

THINK ABOUT IT

Why would the habitable zone be different for each star?

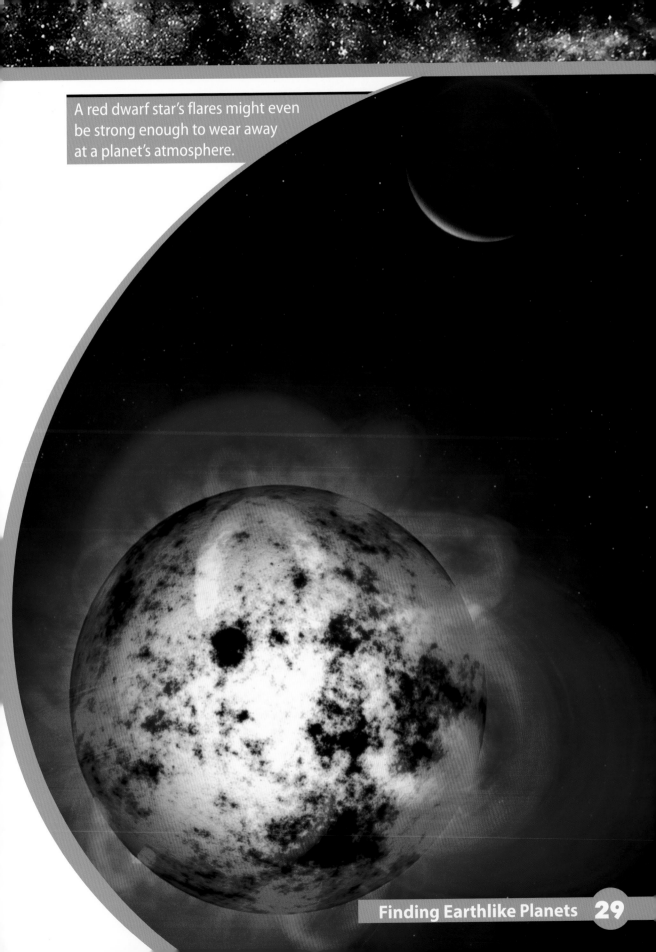

A red dwarf star's flares might even be strong enough to wear away at a planet's atmosphere.

Chapter 5

Don't Forget Moons

Scientists are also searching for earthlike conditions on moons. Moons are smaller rocky bodies that orbit planets. Some moons in our solar system share some characteristics of Earth. For example, Saturn and Jupiter have moons that have both ice and liquid water.

Saturn's moon Enceladus has geysers that spray frozen water. The water in these geysers comes from an ocean under the moon's surface. The geysers break through the moon's surface and spew ice water into space.

Ice water and hydrogen gas sprays from geysers near the south pole of Saturn's moon Enceladus.

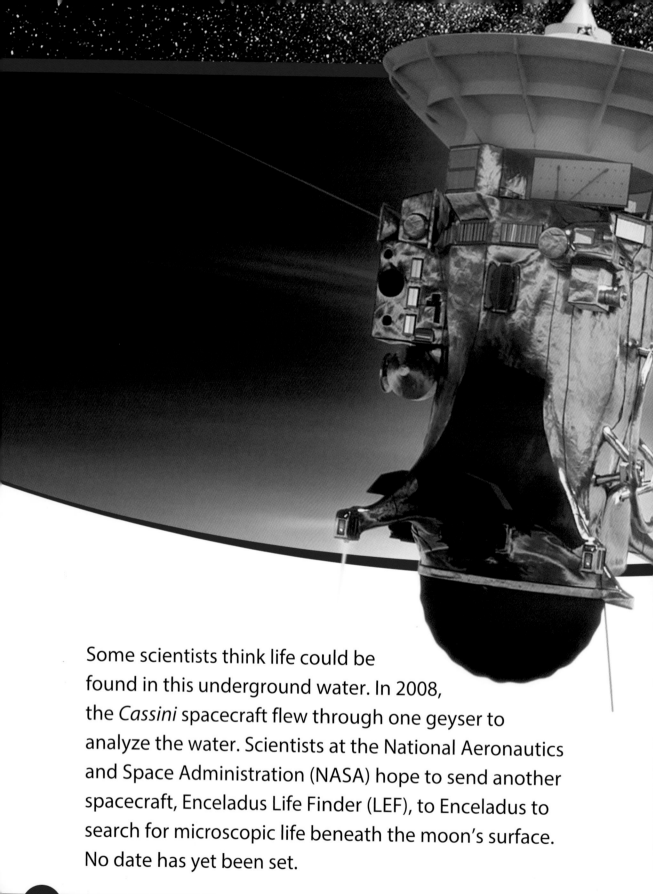

Some scientists think life could be found in this underground water. In 2008, the *Cassini* spacecraft flew through one geyser to analyze the water. Scientists at the National Aeronautics and Space Administration (NASA) hope to send another spacecraft, Enceladus Life Finder (LEF), to Enceladus to search for microscopic life beneath the moon's surface. No date has yet been set.

Cassini launched in 1997 and reached Saturn in 2004. For the next 13 years, it circled the planet. In 2017, it crashed into Saturn, ending its 20-year mission.

Jupiter's moon Europa also has an ocean of water beneath thick sheets of ice. The ice sheets glide on top of the water. Scientists do not know much about Europa yet. But NASA has plans to send a probe, Europa Clipper, to this moon in the 2023s. The probe would carry cameras and other science instruments. It would look for signs of life. The mission might even carry a lander. It could land on Europa and drill into the ice on its surface.

Saturn's moon Titan has some earthlike traits as well. Titan has a thick atmosphere. It even has clouds and lakes. But this moon could not support life. The temperature is far too low for liquid water. So, Titan's lakes are filled with **hydrocarbons** instead. But Titan does have a complex weather system. Hydrocarbons even rain onto the moon's surface. Titan is the only other place in our solar system with a weather system similar to Earth's.

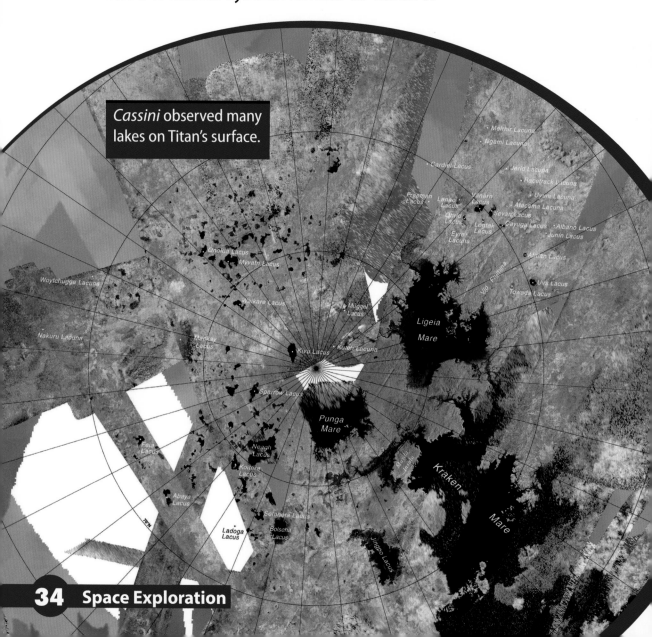

Cassini observed many lakes on Titan's surface.

Scientists are also looking for exomoons, or moons that orbit exoplanets. This search is difficult. An exomoon would be smaller than the planet it orbits. It would reflect less light, making it even harder to see. An exomoon's smaller mass also means it would pull less on the star that its planet orbits. This pull is almost always too small to detect with current telescopes.

Scientists thought they found an exomoon in 2017. However, the signal was hard to see. Not all astronomers are convinced it is an exomoon. Some scientists are looking through information collected by the Kepler space telescope. They hope to see exomoons blocking tiny amounts of light from stars. This search takes a lot of computers working together. Without any examples of exomoons, it is difficult for scientists to know what to look for. But because most planets in the solar system have moons, it is likely that many exoplanets have moons as well.

THINK ABOUT IT

Why might scientists want to study Titan even though the moon is too cold to support life?

Chapter 6

The Planet Next Door

In 2016, scientists found an exoplanet orbiting a star called Proxima Centauri. Proxima Centauri is the closest star to our Sun. It is still so far away that a spaceship traveling at the speed of light would take more than four years to get there. However, there is often much more space between stars. So, two unrelated stars being just a few light-years apart is a relatively short distance.

Proxima Centauri is approximately one-eighth as massive as the Sun.

The exoplanet is known as Proxima b. It is closer to Proxima Centauri than Mercury is to the Sun. But Proxima Centauri is a small star that glows red. The red color means it is not as hot as the Sun. Therefore, Proxima b orbits in Proxima Centauri's habitable zone. The temperature on Proxima b might be perfect for liquid water. Scientists have not actually seen water on Proxima b. But they do know the exoplanet is at least 1.3 times Earth's mass.

Astronomers are excited about Proxima b. Because of how near this exoplanet is to Earth, future telescopes might be able to see some details on the planet. Some scientists even have a plan to study it up close. They want to send several small spacecraft to Proxima Centauri. The spacecraft would have large sails. These sails would reflect light. **Lasers** on Earth would beam light to the spacecraft. This light would bounce off the sails, and the spacecraft would be pushed forward. This new technology is not yet ready. But it would help the spacecraft travel quickly. They could reach Proxima Centauri in only a few decades.

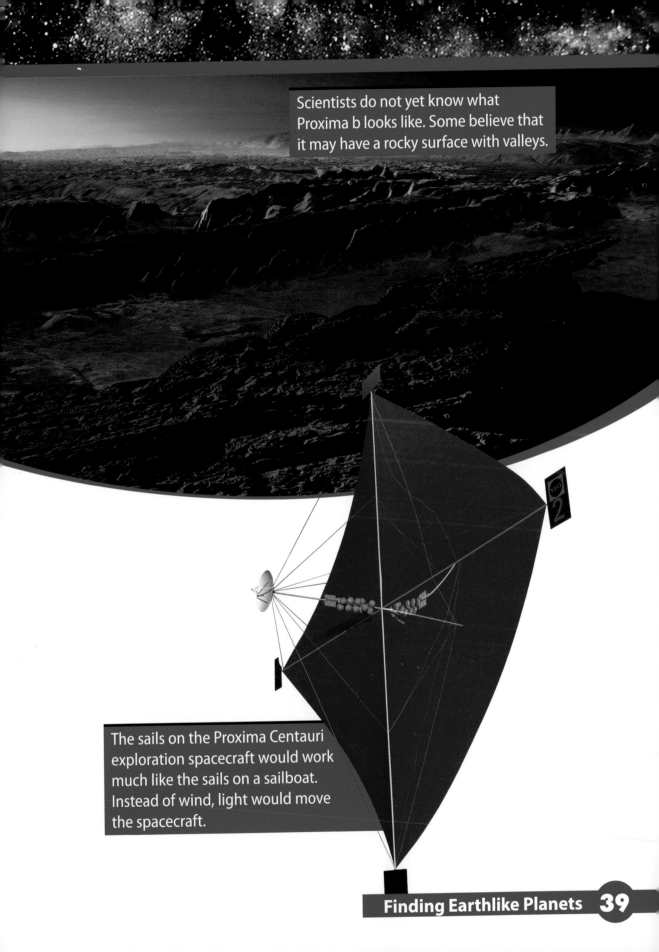

Scientists do not yet know what Proxima b looks like. Some believe that it may have a rocky surface with valleys.

The sails on the Proxima Centauri exploration spacecraft would work much like the sails on a sailboat. Instead of wind, light would move the spacecraft.

In 2017, scientists found TRAPPIST-1. This dwarf star has seven possible earthlike planets in its orbit.

Chapter 7

The Next Steps

Now that scientists have found so many exoplanets, the next step is learning about the planets' details. For example, scientists want to know if exoplanets have oceans of water or thick atmospheres. Current telescopes cannot detect these details yet. To see the planets' surfaces, scientists need to use more advanced telescopes.

NASA has plans for several new space missions to search for exoplanets. In April 2018, it launched Transitory Exoplanet Survey Satellite (TESS) to explore the most distant parts of space. In 2020, the James Webb Space Telescope will be launched. It will replace the Hubble Space Telescope. Then, in 2026, the European Space Agency will launch Planetary Transits and Oscillations (PLATO) to search for habitable exoplanets with liquid water.

Around 2025, NASA has plans for another telescope called Wide-Field Infra Red Survey Telescope (WFIRST). This is designed to look across the entire sky. Scientists could use WFIRST to learn about exoplanets' atmospheres. WFIRST will be designed to measure the chemicals in exoplanets' atmospheres. In May 2018, WFIRST entered its initial design phase. Other proposed missions involving telescopes include HabEx, Lynx, Origins Space Telescope (OST), and LUVOIR (Large UV/Optical IR Surveyor). The purpose of all these missions is to gain more information about possible exoplanets.

Astronomers believe these new missions will find thousands of exoplanets. As more exoplanets are discovered within stars' habitable zones, the odds of finding an earthlike planet increase.

THINK ABOUT IT

From the time the first exoplanets were discovered until today, how has technology affected the search for earthlike planets?

TESS will continue the search for exoplanets. It will cover an area 400 times larger than Kepler once observed.

Starshades

Some astronomers hoped to send a starshade into space with WFIRST. The starshade would fly in front of the telescope and block the light of faraway stars. The starshade would be shaped like a giant disk with petals. Each petal would be covered in gold-colored plastic. These petals would reflect starlight away from the telescope.

Stars are much brighter than their exoplanets. Blocking light from stars would make it easier for the telescope to pick up light reflected from nearby exoplanets. Scientists are testing small starshades in labs on Earth. They use lasers to mimic starlight. They are even coming up with ways to send a starshade the size of a football field into space.

Light from exoplanets may help scientists determine if an exoplanet has an atmosphere. Eventually, scientists may be able to tell if a planet's atmosphere contains water or oxygen. These details would help scientists search for an Earth twin and even look for signs of life on other planets.

Quiz

1 What are three traits of an Earth twin?

2 What are habitable planets called?

3 What was the date of the discovery of the first exoplanet?

4 Why would blocking light from stars make it easier to detect exoplanets?

5 What is the name of the research group that John Asher Johnson leads?

6 What was the length of the Kepler space telescope?

7 When was the Hubble Space Telescope launched?

8 How many exoplanets had been identified by 2018?

Answer: 1. Answers should include size, density, rockiness, presence of water, dry land, or atmosphere. **2.** Goldilocks planets **3.** 1992 **4.** Starlight can conceal the dimmer light from exoplanets. **5.** ExoLab **6.** 15.3 feet long (4.7 m) **7.** 1990 **8.** 3,800

Key Words

atmosphere: the layers of gases that surround a planet or moon

dense: relatively heavy or massive for its size. Density is calculated by dividing an object's mass by its volume

diameter: a straight line through the center of a circle or sphere that connects its opposite sides

gravity: the attractive force between two objects that is due to their masses and affected by how far apart they are

hydrocarbons: substances that contain only carbon and hydrogen. Titan's surface has the hydrocarbons methane and ethane in liquid form

lasers: devices that produce a very intense, narrow beam of light

massive: having a large mass, a measurement of how much physical matter an object contains. Mass is related to, but not the same as, weight

orbiting: repeatedly following a curved path around another object because of gravity

probe: a device used to explore

radius: a straight line from the center of a circle or sphere to its edge

Index

Log on to www.av2books.com

AV² by Weigl brings you media enhanced books that support active learning. Go to www.av2books.com, and enter the special code found on page 2 of this book. You will gain access to enriched and enhanced content that supplements and complements this book. Content includes video, audio, weblinks, quizzes, a slideshow, and activities.

AV² Online Navigation

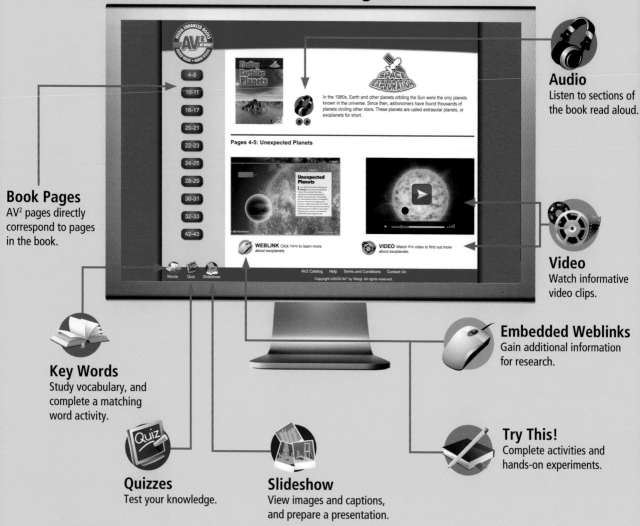

Audio
Listen to sections of the book read aloud.

Book Pages
AV² pages directly correspond to pages in the book.

Video
Watch informative video clips.

Key Words
Study vocabulary, and complete a matching word activity.

Embedded Weblinks
Gain additional information for research.

Quizzes
Test your knowledge.

Slideshow
View images and captions, and prepare a presentation.

Try This!
Complete activities and hands-on experiments.

AV² was built to bridge the gap between print and digital. We encourage you to tell us what you like and what you want to see in the future.

Sign up to be an AV² Ambassador at www.av2books.com/ambassador.